The Boost Circuit

A Modern Guide to Building a Better Business

THE BOOST CIRCUIT

The Boost Circuit

A Modern Guide to Building a Better Business

by:
Jesse D Poole

edited by:
Corey C. Poole

BOOST CIRCUIT INC.
Natchitoches, Louisiana 71457

www.boostcircuitinc.com

For my loving wife Corey and our children Jessica and Jaydon. Without their support I could not have accomplished any of this.

Foreword

This is a guide for today. The current state of business is constantly changing. Change is inevitable. The problem I've seen is that lately business owners have failed to keep up. Everyone wants to know where success starts. It starts with a hunger to evolve, change, and grow. It starts with a need to succeed and stay relevant in today's technology driven society. The desire to succeed is powerful. Those of us that have it will channel that desire into intent, which becomes a force to execute the things we must do in order to propel our dreams into reality. The best piece of advice any entrepreneur can give another entrepreneur is: you can do it.

Table of Contents

About The Author   Pg.1

Getting Started   Pg.3

Let's Get Digital   Pg.5

Design   Pg.8

Branding   Pg.10

Brand Communication and Awareness   Pg.14

Brand Quotes   Pg.16

Social Media   Pg.18

Marketing   Pg.21

About the Author

My name is Jesse. I own Boost Circuit Inc., a full service media, entertainment, and digital marketing solutions company that owns and operates digital, mobile, video, and social media properties focused on small to mid-sized markets. The company specializes in the now; creating and distributing original and motivating media experiences that connect communities with the content they love, people they trust, products and services they want, and things that matter.

I'm a husband, father, entrepreneur, designer, business consultant, and digital marketing mastermind. I'm a voice of the generation that is living in this current state of technological evolution and digital reality. I remember telephones when they had cords, Internet when it had to dial in, and I remember Facebook when I had to have a college email address to create an account. I remember waiting through the sounds of a dial up modem, which turned into logging on to access, which turned into a constant state of connectivity.

I've experienced this evolution first hand by keeping up with social media, keeping up with the state of the Internet, keeping up with our leaps and bounds in technology, and how businesses have utilized the Internet and are taking their digital presence to the next level. If you've been lost on how to modernize your business through better branding, proper marketing, and gaining an insight on understanding what the next generation of consumers will expect out of you and your business, this guide is for you.

Getting Started

Starting a business can be a long drawn-out process or it can be a simple, easy, step by step process that opens new doors to being a successful entrepreneur. Under no circumstances at any point throughout this book do we suggest, imply, or insist that everything can be done without legal, financial, or professional consultation. This is merely a guide to helping entrepreneurs and business owners take advantage of the digital age of marketing, branding, and design that has hindered businesses in the past that didn't have the luxury of the internet, social media, and access to a plethora of knowledge, insight, guidance, and tools that when utilized; can lead to success.

If you haven't ever set out to open a business, always check with your Secretary of State or visit a local SBA office to discuss your intent. Once you've figured out what services or goods you'll be in business to sell and decided what you want to call your business, it's time to make sure the business name is available. Think about the services or goods you'll be selling. Choosing a business name can be the most difficult part of getting started if you get hung up on forcing a clever or unique name. Be creative but don't overthink it. The name won't make or break the business. The customer experience will be more important. You can do most of this with your Secretary of State and in most cases online. You'll want to speak to an accountant and/or lawyer during this process too.

Deciding what type of business is important to decide before beginning. If the business name you want is available it's time to start the filing process. Some states take longer than others so be patient with the paperwork. While you wait to get your initial filing done and your Articles of Organization, it's a good time to start thinking about the next steps to ensure you are on the right path to success.

Let's Get Digital

Anyone can build a website and create a social media page. Not everyone can build a digital presence that delivers results. That takes time, patience, and practice. In today's market you need several things: better branding, proper marketing, and a strong digital presence that engages consumers, targets potential clients, and reaches a vast demographic. You need increased visibility, a professional brand, and an up-to-date website that's optimized for mobile, tablet, and desktop devices.

Some search engines don't show your website in their search results if it's not optimized for viewing on mobile devices. Over half of all website traffic happens on a mobile device these days. Mobile website traffic is higher than ever and continues to grow. If your website isn't useable on a mobile phone or tablet, you're losing business to your competitors.

Most adults have their mobile phone within arms reach 24 hours a day, 7 days a week. To stay connected to this demographic, you need a social media platform that interacts with clients and fans and speaks to the community. Allowing your audience to stay connected to what matters, the things they love, and the services they need is an important part of a successful business.

An online presence is critical for your business now more than ever. This is where your business gains credibility and where consumers learn about you, your products and your services. It takes less than two seconds to form a first impression upon entering a website. Updated designs increase conversions by appealing to a consumer's sense of trustworthiness and reliability. If a consumer feels they can trust and rely on your business for the products and services they need, your business can convert their visit to your website or social media accounts into a viable relationship. If they trust and rely on you for what they need, they'll continue to bring you business. Not only that; they'll recommend you to their friends and family. Conversions can transform into a consistent stream of revenue for your business.

Updated designs also maintain your business' professionalism. No one would walk into a broken-down, dismal storefront. In a very real sense, your digital presence (your website and social media accounts) are your storefront. The look and feel of your website goes a long way toward lending your business credibility and gaining an audience to convert traffic into crucial new business.

Design

Having an online presence is a good first step, but it won't be truly effective unless there's an overall solid appearance. Design is one of the most important parts of your business. Your image matters. In today's visually oriented society, if you're not doing the best job you can to brand your business in a way that sets you apart from your competition, you're missing out on potential growth.

Your logo, business cards, ads, letterheads, store front and signage should match. Consistent branding is crucial.

Your website and social media accounts are the digital face of your business. Visitors decide within seconds in they are interested in working with your company, just as they decide within a few feet of your physical location if they will have a good experience. A professional look and feel for your digital presence will lend credibility to your business.

Strive for two main things in a design: simplicity and clarity. Keep your logos, cards, and advertisements simple and to the point. However, remember that there's no reason to make them plain and boring. Finding a middle ground between "overdone" and "way outside the line" is key.

Branding

A brand is a name or term, a design or symbol, that sets you apart from your competition. Branding is said to have begun in ancient Egypt. They would brand livestock in the mid 2,000s BC to separate their livestock from another person's.

Your brand is your value. It's your promise to the consumer. The better your brand, the more effective it will be.

After you've designed a logo and developed a style guide, sticking to it is the next most important thing in the branding process. If you change your logo every few months the public will never associate your business with a logo that's memorable.

In today's fast-paced mobile driven society, if you aren't branding your business consistently, consumers may not be certain of your ability to deliver the products or services you offer. This may lead to them questioning your legitimacy. Your design is part how you carry yourself and part how you're viewed by consumers.

The way the public views you is important, but you should also be concerned with how you view yourself. Your logo, slogans, and signage is part of it but your logo is not your brand. Your brand is what's said about you and your business when you aren't in the room. It's how you're thought of. You can shape and mold your brand, but it's ultimately up to the consumers, employees, and your peers to have the final say in how it's perceived.

You have four main factors associated with your brand's identity:

1. Attributes: A set of ideals/labels you want to be associated with.
2. Benefits: Communicated through your attributes, the benefits are physical and emotional translations.
3. Values: Symbolizing your core specific values attracts like minded individuals who share the same values.

4. Personality: This is the most important factor: humanizing your brand. You can describe a successful brand identity as if it were alive. Building and maintaining a long-lasting relationship with consumers gives them a sense of personal interaction with the brand. Your personality drives consumers to understand the benefit of working with you.

Brand elements are another set of factors to consider when developing your brand. A combination of the elements can be Trademarked (™). Going through the process to register your trademark on a state level, at minimum, is encouraged.

- name: the word or words used to identify a company, product, service, or concept

- logo: the visual trademark that identifies a brand

- tagline or catchphrase

- graphics

- shapes

- colors

- sounds

- scents

- tastes

- movements

Don't be afraid to try new logos in this initial stage of business development. They can evolve as you grow into what you want your business to become. Pictured below is a visual representation of how Boost Circuit's logo evolved over the first few months during the branding process.

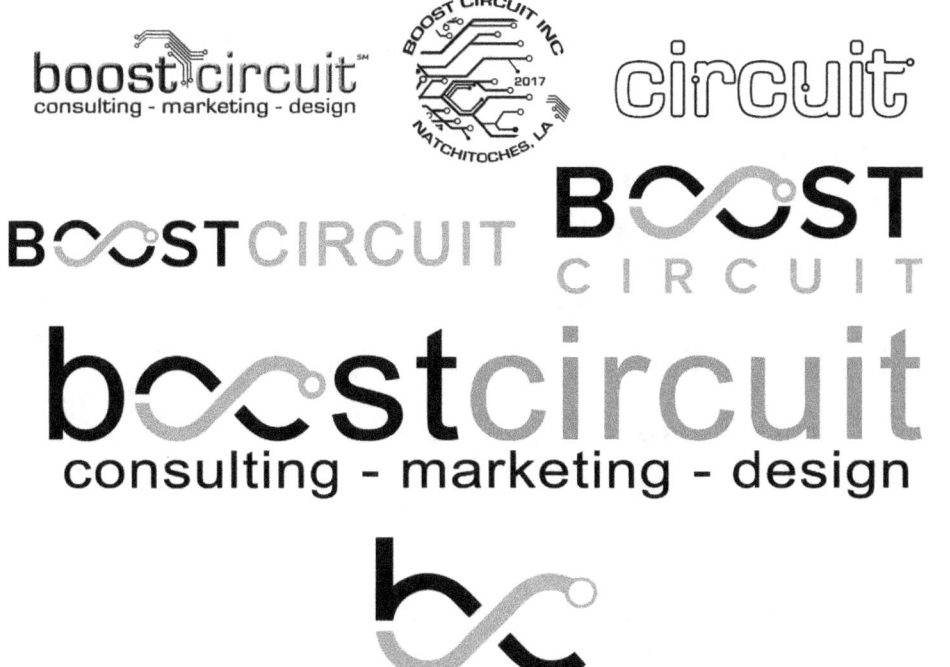

Brand Communication and Awareness

You have a brand, now you have to build awareness. Brand recognition is the first phase. Brand awareness is centered around a consumer's ability to easily remember, recall, and recognize your brand, logos, and the brand's advertising. This is the main step in consumers' purchasing decision processes. Awareness is converted into purchases. Most often, consumers won't consider buying a brand they're unaware of. Their awareness is a key component in gauging and understanding the effectiveness of your brand identity and its ability to communicate the value of your products and services.

Aim for "Top-of-Mind" awareness: A consumer's ability to almost subconsciously recall a brand when asked about a product or service category.

Brand identity is collectively the most fundamental asset to your brand's equity. Without communication, your identity becomes obsolete. Integrated Marketing Communications relates to the clarity of a consistent message. These five components make up IMC:

1. Advertising

2. Public relations

3. Personal Selling

4. Direct Marketing

5. Sales Promotion

Brand Quotes

"Your brand is what other people say about you when you're not in the room."

-Jeff Bezos, Founder of Amazon.com

"Your premium brand had better be delivering something special, or it's not going to get any business."

-Warren Buffet, CEO of Berkshire Hathaway

"Too many companies want their brands to reflect some idealized, perfected image of themselves. As a consequence, their brands acquire no texture, no character, and no public trust."

-Richard Branson, Founder of Virgin Group

"Focus on building the best possible business. If you are great, people will notice and opportunities will appear."

-Mark Cuban, Owner of Dallas Mavericks

"Design is not just what it looks like and feels like. Design is how it works."

-Steve Jobs, Co-Founder of Apple

"If your business is not a brand, it's a commodity."

-Donald Trump, President of The Trump Organization

"If people believe they share values with a company, they will stay loyal to the brand."

-Howard Schultz, CEO of Starbucks

Social Media

Some businesses are still neglecting this absolutely simple, amazingly useful branding, marketing, and advertising tool. Being active on social media grows your referral business, engages customers, and builds a sense of community. It supports every one of your marketing efforts.

Social media humanizes your brand. Being authentic in a world full of digital mediums is one of the most important things you can do. If your company doesn't have any social media accounts, you're losing credibility. Social media is now a part of our everyday lives. With social media your business maintains a direct line of access to interact with consumers.

You can keep up with and see at a glance growth, engagement, and reach. Maintaining continuity across multiple platforms supports your efforts toward creating an effective brand. Consumers are more likely to use a local business if it's available on social media and has plenty of information. Reviews and testimonials also help.

Shoppers' buying decisions are heavily influenced by social media. Most Facebook users prefer to connect with their favorite brands on Facebook. This is still the number one platform to engage consumers, fans, and friends. Twitter and Instagram are the next two largest social media platforms and growing fast is Snapchat, which continues to roll out new branding features and advertising for businesses. Snapchat will certainly be a game changer in the next few years.

These questions should be asked:

• Are you engaging your network?

• Are you reaching consumers?

• How extensive is your influence?

Here are some things to think about when you dive into social media, on any platform:

Consistency: Never use more than one profile for multiple accounts. You want your clients, colleagues, and fans to find you. Your logo should match your sign just as much as your logo should be your business's profile photo.

Covers/Headers: These should all match. As the platforms evolve, so too does their image size and file type requirements. Keeping up with this is one of the most crucial parts of social media marketing.

One of the many problems business owners have with social media is continuing the effort. Once you start posting, uploading, and sharing, you must maintain a consistent expression of interest in letting the public know you're open and willing to provide them with the services they need. Too often business pages have little to no content, misleading posts, and poorly executed ads. If you use products to showcase your business in your profile photo, and it changes with the seasons, you've missed an opportunity to maintain brand awareness. How can you expect customers to recognize your page in their feed if the profile graphic you use isn't your logo or it's an image that changes too often?

Marketing

After you've situated your digital image and have been consistently branding, you now have to think about combining the branding efforts to increase your reach. Digital marketing on social media is the most powerful tool available, but it's not the only option.

As print mediums become obsolete, there are many online journals and periodicals that publish daily. Exploring such avenues increase the ability for the public to see your brand.

Another great piece of advice is to engage in community projects. Not just by donating time, but by partnering with other businesses and local offices to reach your audience in new ways.

This could be as simple as dropping off physical business cards in places with high traffic, printing your own newsletter or even using social media to ask people to interact at your physical location by showing you ads on their mobile device that displays a "deal of the day." Get creative!

This is a new frontier for everyone. Keep track of your return on investment (ROI) and utilize the efforts that work the best for you.

If it works for your biggest competitor, it can work for you. Follow your competition and mimic their efforts. Not everyone will have the same ideas. This is great for the free market. You have numerous options available to advertise, engage, and communicate with consumers instantly.

Don't give up after a few weeks or even a few months. Building anything takes time, effort, and patience. If it's worth doing, it's worth doing right. Build your brand, target your audience, and engage and interact with fans and followers. Adapt, grow, and evolve as the market changes. Good Luck!